Ready to Cook

by Susan McCloskey

illustrated by
Jackie Snider

MODERN CURRICULUM PRESS
Pearson Learning Group

Hi! My name is Ready Fox. I'm always ready to cook. I'm always ready for a joke too.

This book has lots of jokes, plus a recipe or two. Try them out at home. First make sure your mom or dad says it's okay!

Here's a joke for you.

How are yogurt and vinegar different?

You don't know?

Well, I'll never send you to the store for yogurt!

My first recipe is a great way to
cook chicken.

Put pieces of chicken in plain yogurt.
Keep it in the refrigerator for two hours.
Then bake the chicken, with a grown-
up's help. The sauce will taste so good!

(Be sure to wash your hands after you
touch chicken that has not been cooked!)

She wanted to grow mashed potatoes!
Lots of people cook mashed potatoes
for dinner. Here's how to make them
better. Stir in a little bit of brown mustard.
Then take a bow as you serve them!

What did the octopus have for lunch?

A peanut butter and jellyfish sandwich!
Do you ever get tired of plain old
peanut butter and jelly? Skip the jelly. Mix
applesauce and marshmallow cream with
the peanut butter. Trust me! You'll love it!

How can you tell if an elephant has been in the refrigerator?

Look for elephant tracks in the cream cheese!

Here's a good sandwich to make. You can take it to school. Spread cream cheese on bread. Add sunflower seeds. Apples are good too. Yum!

How can you keep your eyes from hurting
when you drink cocoa?

Take the spoon out of the cup, silly!
Cocoa can warm you up on a cold day.
To make it really good, add a drop of vanilla.

How do you catch a speeding horse?

Stand behind a tree and make a noise like oats! Ha ha!

Horses love oats. Lots of people eat them too.

You can make hot cereal taste yummy. Make a little well in the center. Then add honey or syrup. Now that's special!

What did the cook say when the waffles
fell on the floor?

"Oh, how waffle!"

No one will say that when you try my recipes. Instead, they'll say, "Oh, how yummy!"

Have fun cooking!